Sooooo… You Want To Be "A" MANAGER!

Things You Should Know!

I0487632

Rick Godfrey

TRAFFORD

© Copyright 2005 Rick Godfrey.

All rights reserved. No part of this publication may be reproduced, stored in a retrieval system, or transmitted, in any form or by any means, electronic, mechanical, photocopying, recording, or otherwise, without the written prior permission of the author.

Note for Librarians: a cataloguing record for this book that includes Dewey Decimal Classification and US Library of Congress numbers is available from the Library and Archives of Canada. The complete cataloguing record can be obtained from their online database at:

www.collectionscanada.ca/amicus/index-e.html

ISBN 1-4120-4191-0

TRAFFORD

Offices in Canada, USA, Ireland, UK and Spain

This book was published *on-demand* in cooperation with Trafford Publishing. On-demand publishing is a unique process and service of making a book available for retail sale to the public taking advantage of on-demand manufacturing and Internet marketing. On-demand publishing includes promotions, retail sales, manufacturing, order fulfilment, accounting and collecting royalties on behalf of the author.

Book sales for North America and international:

Trafford Publishing, 6E–2333 Government St.,

Victoria, BC v8t 4p4 CANADA

phone 250 383 6864 (toll-free 1 888 232 4444)

fax 250 383 6804; email to orders@trafford.com

Book sales in Europe:

Trafford Publishing (uk) Ltd., Enterprise House, Wistaston Road Business Centre,

Wistaston Road, Crewe, Cheshire cw2 7rp UNITED KINGDOM

phone 01270 251 396 (local rate 0845 230 9601)

facsimile 01270 254 983; orders.uk@trafford.com

Order online at:

www.trafford.com/robots/04-1998.html

10 9 8 7 6 5 4 3 2

The Author
R.G. (Rick) Godfrey

Husband – Father – Prior Executive with TRW and Honeywell - Currently Chairman of MRI. He also served the United States Department of Defense as a member of the Defense Manufacturing Board and the Defense Science Board.

This book was written for his children. Each time they called for free consulting advice on their jobs and careers they asked questions on "how to do this and how to do that". Later they began to ask questions on management and the techniques of being a successful manager. This caused him to build a file from his answers to their questions and the recalling of his own past experiences and all of this formed the skeleton for this book. May they and others use this material in good health and continued enjoyment for effective management of their businesses and careers!

He is now retired and living in Washington State on the Olympic Peninsula. From here he does fishing, crabbing, clamming and consulting on profit and loss turn-arounds, re-engineers organizations and their cultures and still spends some time mentoring his children in their careers in California, Texas and Sweden. His favorite projects still deal with people and their needs throughout their careers. He also enjoys leading teams for "acquisition due diligence reviews" for United States and International corporations.

Sooooo... You Want To Be "A" Manager!

Things You Should Know!

Contents

"Proposition:"

Lots of people are born.
--Few excel at leading others!

Chapter 1.   <u>WHY?</u>

Where does the energy and drive come from for those of us who want to be managers? It is certainly not a birthright or something that comes stamped on your birth certificate or passport. What makes some of us want to do this job? Taking the responsibility for the performance of others is an awesome task. Some folks will do almost anything to avoid responsibility for other people, making decisions and guiding other employees' to their individual results! The ability to lead and motivate others is the essence of "Managing".

I can speak only for myself when I say that it was, and is always exciting and rewarding to help other people accomplish their goals and achieve their personal expectations. Notice that I did not say easy. The road one chooses when deciding to become a manager is a little more lonely than traveling in a group under the cover of numbers of people. I suppose that this was the genesis of the phrase "the buck stops here".

Managers are born
<u>and then</u> grown

There are many points of view about when a manager is born and how one is developed. Some say this happens when times are tough; others say during a crisis. Some say it is a matter of progression and some day you wake up to find out you are a manager and do know how to direct people and get results through others. One thing is pretty clear. No two managers are exactly alike.

There is no cookie cutter for stamping out managers. We all develop our skills over periods of time in which we are faced with many different challenges and situations. As we work our way through all of these events we acquire additional skills or tools to do the job as a manager. It takes time, energy, education, training and lots of other elements like practical experience to become a good manager. It takes even greater skills to become a great manager. Some people subscribe to the philosophy that good managers can be developed over time with learning and teaching. Others of us are of the opinion that great managers are developed during hard and tough times. In fact, I feel that great managers <u>can</u> be developed through adversity, especially when these lessons are blended with the experiences gained during a number of business cycles over time. One business cycle does not make a complete manager. One thing is for sure – no great manager was ever developed that I know of – sitting in a classroom!

It has been my experience that the best managers are developed during the "hard-time business cycles." When the sales or revenue growth trends turn flat or even shrink, you must bring all your skills to the management table and then begin to develop processes and game plans to operate the business under duress and in uncharted and turbulent business environments. You cut personnel, reduce expenses, and generally cut down on any and all areas of expenditure in the budgets. In my mind, this time of difficult situations in the business world is the time when new and great managers develop and demonstrate their true capabilities. It is also the time when the organization recognizes a manager's true value.

This book is NOT meant to be a compendium of everything a person needs to know to be a manager. Rather, it is a personal account, based on decades of experience, of lessons learned that might be useful to someone just starting out in a management career. It is meant to supplement, not replace other management education material. Hopefully it highlights some of the more critical and significant elements that make a difference in how well a manager performs.

Some Say:

"When all is said and done, more is said than done"

--Lou Holtz

Others Say:

"Performance is the art of doing things like you said you would do them" --Rick Godfrey

I Am Happy To Say:

My delightful task has always been to lead people to where they should be going, having them bring with them what they were charged to accomplish, and getting them there when they were supposed to be there.

This is called management!

It's the mark of a leader!

Chapter 2.   LEADERSHIP

Where do good leaders come from?

What makes a good leader successful?

We don't know all the answers BUT we do have some very good role models to refer to when evaluating the people who are successful at being managers. Here are some of the special skills and other attributes that great managers possess:

Team Player
Power Sharer
Gives Credit Where Earned
Good Time Management
Good Listener
Analytical Mind
Asks Good Questions
Seeks Council From Others
Good Communicator
Action Orientated
Compassionate
Resourceful
Thinks Ahead
Leads by Example
Plans for Contingencies
Accepts Responsibility
Listens to Criticism
Caring Individual

Good managers seem to do these things automatically. Some people must have grown up practicing some of these skills but many managers learned early in their careers that practicing these things produces outstanding results. Many of us found early in our management careers that people respond to these skills. Once you discover that people like to be treated fairly and openly, you are on your way to success as a manager. Being a good manager is **ALL** about being a good leader. People inherently want to be part of a winning team and will follow a manager that makes them all feel and look like winners.

A few key things to remember:

-Success does breed continual and additional success.

-People will follow leaders who treat them like they want to be treated. This usually means being treated fairly.

-Sharing of power and giving credit where credit is due always wins trust and respect.

-Give up the "small things" that will make no difference at the end of the day.

-Concentrate on the "big stuff and key things" that affect everyone and their careers or livelihood.

Chapter 3   SUPERVISION
--- SOME HARD STUFF

The fact is, that most of us are very apprehensive and often somewhat nervous when dealing with the "firsts" of our new job responsibilities as the new supervisor/manager. Suddenly everyone expects you to know what to do, how to do it and when to stop and go on almost any subject. **The facts are -- no one gave you a guidebook on how to handle all the situations you will face as a new manager**. In fact, most of us are not given a briefing on the people we are to manage; we are just expected to know how to manage people's grievances, paycheck errors, insurance benefits, vacation entitlements, and hundreds of other things that happen every day in the business world and working environment. And, while we are at it ------- keep the business running at 150% efficiency (whatever that means in your company).

The boss dictates the "pecking order" or organizational power in a firm, and this does not always correlate with your personal performance track record. His/her (the boss) actions, body language, reward systems and their personal actions dictate who has the power to change things and rule the company's internal work processes. Good performance is tolerated but not always appreciated by the entire organization. So you need to make sure that you as a manager do your share of recognition of the valuable contributions made by your employees. Don't rely on your boss (or the human resource department) to do this for you. By the way **---- have**

you read the personnel files of all your employees? If not, you are missing a valuable source of information on how your employees are viewed by the organization. Previous managers' job performance write-ups tend to reflect not only their own views on employee performance but also the views of others in the organization.

Power Sharing. It is very hard for new managers to catch the <u>very significant</u> thought that the sharing of his/her power as a boss creates power within the organization and sometimes in the entire company. People like to be treated as individuals and persons of importance. They also appreciate being trusted in their work. Sharing our power and authority as managers creates dramatic results without compromising the notion of "who's in charge". Honest and sincere praise is never out of vogue and is always appreciated by the people who have earned it. New managers do not always see that power sharing and praising of employees leads people to want to take risk and accomplish more than they ever thought they could do on the job. Often this leads to individuals beginning to demonstrate their capacity for future leadership. The manager who gives up "turf and status" when he/she does not need it are seen by other managers as a "valuable friend and forward thinking manager". In short, this is "power sharing" for the mutual benefit of all.

Some things are not taught directly but rather learned by example. How you manage sets the example for the organization to learn and emulate. You don't need to practice being a supervisor for 10-20 years before you take the chance that individuals have growth potential too. Let them demonstrate it. The ship won't sink if they make one mistake. Instead – **teach them to ask for help <u>BEFORE</u> the ship goes down!** We learn and modify our directions through mistakes.

PRESENTATIONS -----Some advice: avoid mountains of presentation material when you first become a manager. Use only enough to cover the point correctly. Usually you can tell how much trouble a manager is having creating positive results by the number of presentation slides he/she brings to the meeting. The more slides a manager brings to a meeting – the more trouble he/she is likely to be in – or get in by making an unfocused presentation! Keep it simple and straightforward. Plant the thought – make the point – draw a conclusion and sit down. The longer the explanation – the more questions will be raised and asked. Questions will follow IF they are important and needed. Constructive assessments will also be forthcoming it they are needed.

THREE MAJOR EVENTS IN THE LEARNING CURVES OF DEVELOPING NEW MANAGERS:
<u>Hiring</u> -- the time when you find out if **YOU** know what **YOU** are looking for in a person's capabilities and character.
<u>Discipline</u> -- the time when **YOU** find out if **YOU** have prepared your case properly.
<u>Firing</u> – the time when **YOU** find out if **YOU** have managed well and have done the right things for your employee and your organization.

Firing: This may be the final event in your relationship with this one employee. Learn from it! Don't waste it!

So many managers fail to understand their real responsibilities in the coaching and developing of people. Done properly, this coaching produces results in business. Young managers sometimes think the employee is totally responsible for individual actions and results. This is **only true if you have prepared the employee** for such responsibilities. Did you explain the job's responsibilities -- not just the tasks? Did you give feedback to the employee on how he/she was performing against the job's assigned tasks? Have you done this more than once? Have you ever given a performance review that lets the employee feed back his/her perspective and feelings about the job? Did you ask for comments on your coaching and teaching skills to improve his or her performance? This "give and take" during the review process is where you really lean the inner feelings of an employee and how you are perceived as a manager through the eyes of an employee.

The **"YOU"** in the above statements of Hiring, Discipline and Firing is really a major, major element in your understanding the role you have in developing your skills to become a great manager. The preparation for these three events is really a report card on you as a manager and a leader. Your management skills will take a great leap forward, or backward, depending on how well you have prepared for these events. The lessons learned during these three process events will stay with you forever.

When you look into the eyes of your employee (and you better be looking into their eyes during the above three events) it suddenly occurs to you that this may be *THE ONLY TIME THAT YOU GET SOLID CONFIRMATION THAT YOU HAVE MADE THE CORRECT ASSESSMENTS AND FINAL DECISIONS* concerning his/her future career with your company. *A few key observations worth remembering during periods of high stress and employee performance concerns:*

"The leadership role is a constant search for improvement. Being a leader is not easy, but it's very rewarding when it begins to bear the fruit from your efforts."

"Leadership is the key to positive change in an organization's development and maturity."

"Developing quality processes and making cultural changes are just plain hard work."

"Cultures change slowly -- People are the key to any permanent change. "

"Managers, like other employees, have a responsibility to the company. its customers, its shareholders and the employees to always be professional."

"Go fishing once in awhile - it's good for the sole!"

Chapter 4.   HIRING

"Your one-time chance to acquire a great employee"

Interesting that anyone would ever consider entering into an interview before writing down the criteria for a good candidate. Sometimes we begin interviews before we have even developed a valid job description. Imagine buying a car without any procurement specifications or personal criteria? Not me!

Once again --- running a good interview and hiring process takes good managerial preparation time and effort – this is commonly known as work. Companies often have descriptions but they tend to be very generalized. Also, don't take the "short-cut" of using an old outdated job description--- you will short change all the parties involved. Doing an updated written job description forces you as a manager to think and provides a "standard" for the new employee and his/her job.   Additionally, it requires you as the manager to do self-examination on the job skills being sought in the new applicant. If this is done properly you will also give the job description to a personnel department to validate the pay scale for the job. Sometimes we pay too little salary or too much because the job requirements have changed from the last time we hired someone into this job. Finally, the written job description becomes the yardstick against which we will measure performance in the future.

Some managers only hire persons who match their own personality, skills, and interest levels. This is sometimes easy and fun but does not always create the most advantages for the company or yourself. Often it is very advantageous to hire people with skills in areas where your personal background and skill set is weak. This hiring of skills that you yourself are weak or deficient in, strengthens the whole team and gives opportunity for future growth. Remember, you may be hiring your own replacement.

Lastly --- don't be afraid to ask about the candidate's previous employment record, reasons for departures, criteria for answering the ad for your job, etc. Too often managers get "cold feet" during the interview on asking questions about the interviewee's background and reasons for changing employers. If you don't seek out this data during the interview --- when are you going to find out about the person's background – after they are hired and then must be terminated for cause? When you finish the interview you should know all you need to know to make the hiring decision except for one fact --- the background check with his/her former employer. Some managers fail to do this and later find that the previous employer has the candidates file marked "not eligible for rehire." This is a real red flag on the previous employment history. Frankly, if I found this candidate's file marked "not eligible for rehire" I would be hard-pressed to hire the individual candidate without some special circumstances. This technique by previous employers is used to keep out of lawsuits and/or other punitive compensation being sought by the candidate from their former employer. Finally, invite the candidate to call back if they have questions about your job or the company itself. Some of us think about additional questions <u>after</u> we leave the interview.

Today it is common practice for former employers (companies) to severely limit the amount of information that they will share with prospective employers. This may make it harder – but no less important – to talk to several references candidly, and to seek their honest opinions about the strengths and weaknesses of candidates you are considering for employment. You should prepare for your conversations with references with the same care that you should use to prepare for good interviews with prospective employees.

Have you ever had "the team of peers" conduct interviews? In organizations that work in a self-directed team environment it is very positive and helpful to have the potential peer employees of the candidate's potential team group do interviews, too. This re-enforces the criteria for the open job with all employees and allows the current employees to "buy into" the new employee's career as he/she joins the company. You will see how very important this "buy-in" is if the new employee has trouble getting into the new job – current employees will help the new employee become successful because they have some "ownership of the person" from the interview process and subsequent hiring.

Chapter 5.   PERFORMANCE APPRAISALS

**Everyone wants to know where they stand
or -- they should want to know!**

**Have you had a performance review in six
months -- one year -- never???**

**This process of letting employees know where they
"stand" is one of the most important tasks and
responsibility you have as a manager.** Probably one
of the most misunderstood concepts in individual
performance reviews is that some managers and
employees think this process is a one-way
transmission without feedback. **It must be a two-
way process to be successful and fruitful.** I have
had a performance review where the boss assumed
the right to be on "transmit" for an hour or two.
Maybe this style was good for the boss' ego but
frankly it was a waste of my time after the first 10
minutes.   The real solid value in a two-way
performance review is to present several (or at least
two) points of view on the employee's level of
performance. Following this two-way discussion
should be the agreement on areas requiring attention
to improve performance. Often companies establish a
"personal improvement plan" for each employee.
This type of detailed performance review sets the
stage for both the employee and the manager to move
to a greater understanding of the work, and
requirements for the employee to advance in the
company. Unfortunately --- sometimes the boss gets
so convinced that he/she is correct on performance
that they don't want to listen to another point-of-view.

The second critical step in a performance review is that it must be written and acknowledged.
Somehow a record must be established for the employee, the company, and even the next boss if you move on to another managerial job and leave the employee with another new manager. All too often a new supervisor/manager inherits employee files with nothing in them but a pay record. Now it becomes a "he said --- she said --- we said" situation with no records to help sort out the real conversations. We all have a tendency to remember what we want to remember about performance conversations. We also have a tendency (a human characteristic) to suppress bad news over time when we are remembering our own performance. Finally, without a written performance appraisal we have no legal documents to back up any employee discipline and /or terminations for "just cause". This last item can become a very expensive cost for the company if there becomes a legal disagreement in the courts of labor law.

Career planning is also a key event for the managers who care about the future of their employees. This important activity helps both the employee and you as a manager prepare for future needs in your organization. If you know someone ultimately wants to move to another group or position, you can prepare them for the job and prepare yourself for the eventual manpower replacement in your own group. A good career plan requires a detailed assessment of the employee's current skills and an appraisal of these skills against the employee's "desired new job". One technique for conducting assessments is to have the employee do a write-up on the job he/she would call optimum for themselves. Having completed this draft then you should have the employee write up an evaluation of their individual talents and skill set in line with this draft. This gives both you and the employee a basis for figuring out what needs to be accomplished before a new career position can be attained. This process should also help make it perfectly clear what your future manpower needs might look like when the current employee departs your group.

Chapter 6.   FIRING AN EMPLOYEE

THE "COUP DE GRACE"

Firing someone is one of the final steps in the development of a complete manager. Some managers never get to this level for several years and some never get the experience at all. The ones who never had to fire anybody -- do not really appreciate the impact that it has on the career of a manager. After firing someone --- you will never manage in exactly the same way in the future. Nowhere will it be so lonely as the closed-door room when you face an employee for termination. Not until the last word is uttered do you (the manager) know if you did the right things with this termination process.

BE PREPARED FOR TEARS, BREAKDOWNS AND BARGAINING FROM THE EMPLOYEE BEFORE THIS EVENT IS OVER.

My first employee discharge was later turned into a success story. The guy could not get to work on time. He constantly overslept and had a job in production control where factory people who depended on him started at 7:00 am. After several counseling sessions (none of which produced the real reason for his constantly being late) I finally had to terminate him for his tardiness. Only at the final moment of our separation meeting did I actually find out what the real problem was. He managed a roller rink at night and closed up shop at 2:00 am every night. He had been trying to survive on three to four hours of sleep each night. About one year later I had a personal telephone call asking me if I would have lunch with him. The purpose of taking me to lunch was to "thank me" for terminating him. He said that managing roller rinks was the thing that he loved and always wanted to do, but with a new baby, house, etc., he did not have the nerve to quit me and manage a roller rink full time. He wanted me to know that it all turned out wonderful and that he was now managing two rinks successfully.

Critical elements to use as a termination checklist are:

Did you do enough homework to support the decision to terminate? Tip: Document each major event or element that contributes to the employee being put on probation or causes you to conclude that termination is appropriate.

Are the facts of the case conclusive and not extracted from hearsay and/or other people's conclusions?

Did you and the employee meet several times to try to correct the deficiency over which this termination is being planned?

Did the employee agree that he/she has had ample time to correct the deficiency in the job and in the workplace?

Do you have a written performance review that ends with the summary statements supporting this termination?

Don't leave this final event to oral input only.
Remember, you may next face this employee in a
labor court where the only testimony that wins the
case is a written one.

**If you answer NO to any of the above questions
you are not properly prepared to conduct this
termination meeting with the employee**.

Don't forget to review any controversial termination
with your human resources organization! Human
resources involvement in terminations not only gives
you another perspective on your decision but also
they can make sure the legal elements are properly
considered and that they are in order. This
transaction deserves your best efforts and undivided
attention in the preparation process for the final
termination meeting with the employee.

Chapter 7.   HUMAN ELEMENTS IN THE BUSINESS ENVIRONMENT

People are the greatest asset you have as a manger.

People (your employees) can make you or break you as a manager. Your care and feeding of this asset is the most important task you have as a manager. They deserve the best supervision that you can provide. They deserve to be heard whenever they feel the need. They should always know how they stand on performance. There is nothing that is "off limits" concerning the business, their role, and their work process and yes, once again --- their performance against some written standards. Treat all of these elements with respect.

Having said all that, it should be noted that **managers are people, too.** Sometimes managers of managers forget this fact and berate subordinates in public. Respect is earned in the management group too. No manager (nor any person for that matter), should be degraded by his/her boss publicly or in front of other people. **Performance appraisals are personal and should be conducted in private**. For example: I worked for a manager who used to charge out on the workplace floor and start to reorganize my work plans whenever his boss or a customer pressured him for action. When I objected to his behavior we found a closed office and "hashed out our disagreements in private". He soon quit this behavior and regularly sought me out in private before any new changes were made in the workplace. Managerial performance appraisals should to be conducted in private and behind closed doors between the manager and his/her boss.

Often managers talk about someone in the organization who is titled "they". You may have heard people say "they do this" or "they did that". Guess what --- We are them and they includes us! When you look in the mirror you will see "them" every time you look. So the conclusion I draw is that "they"(you) are real people too.

A very smart boss told me that when you choose to manage others, you have chosen to stand in the spotlight of the business and the company for which you work. Leadership always works under the spotlight where everyone can see the results --- good or bad. Maybe this is why lots of people don't want to be managers. This is maybe not the picture you had in your mind about being a manager. The good news is you can choose to become a manager --- the other news is that when you make this choice you are also choosing to work in the spotlight where everyone can see the results of your work and leadership capabilities.

It amazes me that success and failure have very similar elements in organizational situations. One manager said it well when he told me, "You meet the same people on the way down the organization, under the process of demotion, that you met on the way up when you were being promoted". The difference is that on the way up in promotions everyone calls you to say congratulations. On the way down in demotions hardly anyone calls you to see if you are

OK. This is sad since in both cases a real person with real feelings is involved. You knew them both.
ADVICE: Always call a demoted manager whom you respect and tell him/her how you are feeling about their demotion situation. They will be very appreciative and never forget your kindness. **This will not be an embarrassing event for you and it will mean a great deal to the person affected.**

Managers set the rules on how we will conduct our business and how the work will be done.
We call these elements of the business - procedures or policies, manufacturing processing, or any other name that establishes "the process by which we conduct our work". **People develop these rules and limits on yields of good or bad**. Many people think of the processes as being "fixed and set in concrete". No changes allowed by anyone – which is foolish. This is very short sighted when you consider the fact that conditions change. New conditions require new rules or guidelines. Bad processes need to be changed and made much more simple. People should not be forced to use processes that make their tasks harder then they need to be. Sometimes policy and procedure authors write rules that have no value. Some people would say automate or eliminate. If they have no value then eliminate them. In fact any effort needs to be considered wasteful and expendable unless it creates value for the firm. Rules and procedures that have no value creation have no place in the process of running our business. No value rules only create frustration and anxiety in the workplace.

Finally, keep in mind that permitting employees who USE the rules to have a voice in creating them (or updating them as conditions change) –whenever possible – is a very good idea. First, participation helps promote "buy in". Second, it provides a means for the best ideas to be brought to light. Allowing "user" employee participation does not mean that YOU as the manager abdicate your responsibility – you can always assert your right to have the final say.

Failure – an experience that none of us enjoy!

Another painful human reaction is the disappointment of failure. This always affects our performance in the work process (and the successful accomplishment of the work of other employees, too). Some times we fail in our work due to outside forces (death in the family, divorces, bankruptcy, etc.) for which we have some responsibility but rarely is it generated through the work place activities. It is also rare that we fix the external problems with our job related processes. I think it is really important for managers to understand that people who have "failures" -- ALL PEOPLE GO THROUGH A RECOVERY PROCESS THAT IS VERY PREDICTABLE. Several people have defined this phenomenon as "the five phases of pain" which are: rejection -- denials -- pain itself -- blame -- and then reconciliation with the parties involved.

What is critical for managers -- is to recognize the existence of this process and what stage an employee is involved in when it happens. A good alert and caring manager can reduce the stress, shorten the period an employee stays in each phase, and in some cases help move the employee from rejection and denial directly into the reconciliation phase. This helps the employee, the department, and anybody else who gets dragged into the corrective action process of the "recovering employee". It's like the disease of alcoholism --- it is hard to start the cure until the individual acknowledges the need. Then they can be really helped onto the road of improvement and dealing with reality.

Don't promote successful individual contributors to managerial responsibilities if they don't want the job or have no interest in managing people. Some great individual contributors have no desire to manage other people. I have known great design engineers who can't manage a picnic for two to a successful conclusion. BUT – they can design electronic circuits that most of us can't even comprehend. Why would you force one of these great thinkers or designers to become a manager if they do not want the job? The greater the pressure on this group – the more shortcuts they take in the design processes to make time for their employee management portions of their job.

This is a bad deal for the employee - the manager - the company - and you as their boss!

Chapter 8.   TEAM-BUILDING & TEAMWORK

We all too often think that being a manager is the job of making **ALL** the decisions. **Although managers are charged with making the final decision – they do not have to work issues and evaluate opportunities in a vacuum**. Involving others who may be affected, as part of a team to evaluate possible corrective actions or solutions is always a wise thing to do. A lot has been written about consensus decision-making and team sponsorship, but even today not everyone practices it. I have found that people, employees, other managers and bosses tend to accept decisions and recommendations where a team of people participated in the final decision BEFORE THE FACT, rather than after the fact. Teamwork develops endorsement of things. Most people can accept <u>fair</u> decisions even when the decisions are not exactly the precise conclusion the individual might have preferred. And, most of us are appreciative of being considered important enough in a controversial issue decision to have been asked for our opinion BEFORE the final decision is taken.

Team building by managers takes some effort and pre-thinking on the part of a manager. You don't just launch a new idea into an open meeting without having some ideas as where you are going with the concept. This means outlining the objectives, concerns and critical elements of implementing a new concept before you start an open-ended discussion on how to implement your idea. Selling of your idea is best accomplished by preparing a short "in-briefing" to get your audience acquainted with your new concept or proposed method for operating the company, business, or department. Some important things to remember here are:

You could follow a meeting outline like:
    1-Definition of concept/subject
    2-Outline of advantages
    3-Concerns or possible issues
    4-Discussion
        But – be brief -- be concise and -- then be seated!

When you hold this briefing! Limit your time on this first discussion so that each person has time to react and speak. Allow some gestation time for the idea to "brew", and then schedule a follow-up session to hear further inputs before you make any final decisions (set this up before you leave this meeting). It probably took you some time to sort out the idea in your own head – so do not expect everyone else to instantly come to a comfortable decision on your idea without doing some thinking time too.

Team building for employee involvement -- One of my favorite team-building exercises is to have other members of the departmental teams participate in interviewing potential new employees. Through this process they develop "buy-in on the new employees" when they participate in this selection process. A good method for doing this is to call the employees together, announce that you will have a new opening, outline the job responsibilities, ask for suggested candidates, and set-up a planned schedule of interviews to follow their suggestions. Always ask for a written assessment on the candidate from the interviewers. Nothing huge –just a few highlights and comments from their interviews.

Another good team activity is to hold open sessions on the processes used to do the work in a department. Many heads are usually better than one in streamlining the workplace and processes by which the work is done in these workplaces. Employees are usually not bashful when given the opportunity to point out things that inhibit their performance on the job or even as a department. The ultimate teaming takes place when a group of people can self appraise their own group's performance in a calm, objective fashion without feeling "put upon" by any of the members in the group.

Chapter 9.   PUBLIC SPEAKING

"Be sincere --- be brief --- be seated!"

One of my college professors was so good on this subject – Dr. Ralph Nichols at the University of Minnesota in the 1950's. His lessons were simple. You learned by doing. He constantly challenged our messages when speaking – and – he took a personal interest in each student's progress to be a better speaker with clear and concise messages. What a teacher!

I don't know where speakers get the idea that speech length is good or volume is important or "volumes of viewgraphs" make the speech great. Some visual aid things do help the comprehension of the presentation. But -- too many detailed things destroy the message and cloud both the listeners' hearing and the speaker's thoughts with non-important stuff.   I personally like to use cartoons. But -- even these can be a negative detraction if not used properly and sparingly. People seem to remember short graphic messages, but the action word here is short not graphics.

I believe short is beautiful and very effective. I think that we can be too brief but never too short. Some subjects are too difficult to comprehend because we make the subject too difficult to understand. A good example is the fact-finding sessions held by engineers when they examine the choices to be considered when choosing solid state electronic processes for manufacturing electronics chip sets. These sessions are way too hard to follow by the average person and many of us can make no appreciable contributions to the forthcoming decisions - as well as wasting our time sitting in such meetings. **Hold technical briefings in separate sessions, not in general management briefings requiring decisions**. Boring graphics, tables, data files and endless reams of paper are showstoppers. A few of the following messages deliver the required important points without writing thousands of words.

Soooooo --- Grade your speech with some of the following ideas:

> **"If you haven't struck oil in the first three minutes --stop boring!"**

> **"Make sure you have finished speaking before your audience has finished listening."**

> **"Your speech need not be eternal to be immortal."**

> **"Talking with no destination is going nowhere."**

Maybe this chapter and section appears too brief, but I have learned that some of the most important speeches ever delivered seemed short to the speaker ---but the audience connected with the message and remembered the facts for days, weeks and even years.

Sooooo -----Some advice: avoid mountains of presentation material when you first become a manager. Use only enough to cover the point correctly. Usually you can tell how much trouble a manager is having creating positive results by the number presentation slides that he/she brings to the meeting. The more slides a manager brings to a meeting – the more trouble he/she is likely to be in – or get in by making an unfocused presentation! Keep it simple and straightforward. **Plant the thought – make the point – draw a conclusion -- and sit down.** The longer the explanation – the more questions will be raised and asked. Good positive questions will follow IF they are important and needed. Constructive assessments will also be forthcoming it they are needed.

Chapter 10.   CULTURES CHANGE SLOWLY

**It is hard work changing a culture that
has existed for years and years.**

**The organizational culture into which new
managers enter their management careers is
constantly changing and will continue to change in
the future.** The role of the middle manager is
different today than it was in the past. Formerly, they
spent their time interpreting upper management's
instructions and then "rolled out the ideas of a few at
the top to the many workers at the bottom." This is
how organizational structures were built and operated
in the past.

Today things are different. With the use of
technology, information networks, computers, etc.,
we can communicate with many, many more people
faster than ever before. We can also provide more
feedback to the organization and individuals much
faster. And ----- we can do it in seconds not days and
weeks. This makes "flatter organizational structures"
possible. This means fewer managers per numbers of
employees and maybe even fewer management levels
in total. This also means that as managers we have an
opportunity to re-invest the salaries of having fewer
managers into our other employees.

**The way to make significant change is through
people** --- by increasing their training – education –
delegation of power – delegation of authority to the
lower levels -- and many, more good things that
empower the employees. In other words, **we can and**

should treat each employee in just the same way we would like to be treated ourselves. Better trained employees means more effective employees who create less errors. Fewer errors means less rework and more productive work --- the first time we perform it. Fewer errors means happy customers who receive fewer defective products or services. What starts out as a cultural change turns into a happy customer situation created by satisfied employees doing better work. Give more responsibility and the associated authority to the employee and guess what --- the employee becomes more responsible. Wow – isn't this what we want to happen? **Isn't this a good management style to emulate??????**

People are still the key!!!!

"A low expectation usually leads to low results."

"Treat everyone in the manner which you wish to be personally treated!"

"Sharing managerial responsibility is easy. Sharing managerial power is where the big benefits are to be found."

"Do things right the first time - on time - all the time."

"Make it happen - make it last!"

Your business and personal ethics are one of your passports to being trusted. Trust is another secret managerial weapon that you want to learn about quickly!

Chapter 11. TELEPHONE CALLS IN THE "MIDDLE OF THE NIGHT" ARE REALLY ORGANIZATIONAL WAKE-UP MESSAGES!

It is always amazing to me that people will call you to talk of significant issues at the most unusual times of the day or night. I remember a telephone call at about midnight from a senior manager who was considering a career change with another company. After two hours of conversation I finally had to remind him that I was getting up in four hours and could be reached at work in the office at 7:00 am. He could come and talk with me there if he so desired.

Since you are a manager – other employees will seek your opinion on salary issues (yours, theirs, and others). Specific salary data should be treated as proprietary, private and should be held in confidence. Each person's wages and their salaries are his/hers alone. Let them talk about their wages if they want to. Your confidant in wage and salary administration is in the personnel department or with your boss in reviews. The local taproom and hoagie sandwich shop is for eating and drinking, NOT settling wage and salary disputes. Salary discussions are always OK with your employees --- behind closed doors and on a one-on-one basis.

It is also always amazing to me that people and employees will change companies without ever having a detailed conversation with their current company and boss. Why would you leap to a brand new company (that you don't know much about) before you take the time to discuss your current or future situation with your current employer? Some people do! Sometimes in our frustration and discomfort we overlook the facts that this situation could possibly be remedied within our own company. Your employees can always change jobs – why not be the kind of manager that spots this situation and help "save" a good employee for your own company – before they depart!

Good employee relations are like having a good marriage – there must be something in the relationship for both parties.

Win – win is sometimes overused as a phrase to describe a deal where both parties get something good from an association or relationship. Good boss/employee relations are developed over time and not just in place automatically through an organization chart. How often have you heard people say, "My boss does not understand"? ----- Maybe you also have heard people say, "My spouse does not understand" --- or my principal – or my banker – or the cop who gave me the ticket!!!?? The heart of the matter is indicating the need for communication and conversation to surface hidden issues and resolve them. The two people with the issue need to talk it through to some conclusion. Spending our days and nights fussing and fuming about an issue that can only be settled by the two people involved and affected --- is not productive time or energy well spent. When this event is in the workplace – nobody benefits from its continuance. *Fix it OR bury it quickly.*

Chapter 12.   MANAGING OTHER MANAGERS

UP --- DOWN --- SIDEWAYS

When the subject of managing comes up – most of us
think about a person in charge of a group of people
with one-on-one relationships. How about the
opportunity to manage other managers or managers in
charge of other groups? How do/should we manage
our boss? How should we manage our peers? These
are all critical skills required as a great manager. In
fact, the higher you rise in a company the more
important these skills become. Managing *among*
other managers is a great skill to develop. **You don't
need to get personal credit for everything!**

A great communicator (Wm. Onchan) used to teach
the philosophy that we all have limited amounts of
management time. There is boss imposed time,
employee imposed time, peer imposed time, and our
own personally imposed management time
requirements. His position was that you needed to
manage, and provide balance between all of these
elements in order to be successful. Managers who
develop this skill of managing their own time
schedules punctually are very valuable as teachers for
all employees, and become excellent role models for
other managers. Accordingly --- **you quickly learn
that you can't do everything yourself but you <u>must</u>
always have time for the really important stuff!**

The boss **will** have his/her time. You **will** meet with
him/her when they want to meet. You **will** address
their subjects of interest. You **will** set goals with the

boss. You can meet these boss imposed requirements **AND** have your own schedules, too, if you handle things correctly. **BUT**, in order to do these things you need to plan for them, get your boss to agree on the review process and time schedules to conduct these reviews. Some bosses want written reports – but you can get prior agreement on how many and when. Some bosses want detailed meetings for reviews, but you can also get agreement on when and where to hold these sessions.

When was the last time you asked a peer manager for advice, opinion, performance critic or anything else? **When was the last time that you offered to help a peer manager accomplish his/her personal objectives**? When was the last time you asked anybody for his or her opinion BEFORE you implemented organizational, or major process changes? Peer managers can give you a "look from the other side of the organization" before you implement controversial changes. Peer managers (when you ask their opinion about change) can help when you have troubles. You will quickly learn which managers to listen to and which ones from which you don't need to seek advice.

OK – so now you know how to manage the boss and your peers! What about when you are managing your direct reporting managers (or their direct reporting managers)? Remember how you felt when you were a first-line manager way back in the very beginning of your managerial career? Remember how you wanted to do some stuff yourself --- you wanted some help from your boss -- AND you had some things or situations where you would have really appreciated your bosses' involvement. Well --- nothing has changed EXCEPT now you are the boss of bosses. Follow your old feelings and you will come out right. Establish goals with clear objectives -- allow the bosses reporting to you to have involvement in setting the performance targets for accomplishment -- provide for a clear review process and time schedule to do the reviews -- require that their reports be in writing --- **NOW STAND BACK AND GET OUT OF THE WAY** so your managers can do their work. Make it clear that he/she knows and feels comfortable in coming to you for help or advice **IF THEY WANT IT**!

There are a couple of rules about managing managers that all new supervisors should practice right from their first day as a manager-----

Rule # 1: SUBORDINATES SHOULD LEARN QUICKLY THAT IT IS ACCEPTABLE (AND EXPECTED!) TO BRING SURPRISES IN THE ON-GOING OPERATIONS OF THE BUSINESS TO THE BOSS. THEY NEED TO LEARN THAT IT IS PERFECTLY ACCEPTABLE TO COME TO THE BOSS FOR HELP WHEN THEY ARE IN BIG "REAL" TROUBLE --- AND --- THEY SHOULD COME TO THE BOSS TO SEEK HELP ---

BEFORE the ship sinks so the problem can be fixed while there is still time to do so!

Rule # 2: Meetings will start on time with or without all the participants. I used to close the door to the conference room about one minute after the posted starting time. We started the meeting on the assigned subject with or without the missing manager or any other person --- including my boss if he was invited. Guess what: invited attendees became more punctual after one or two sessions because of the embarrassment of being late in a closed session.

Rule # 3: " Don't have too many major rules or they lose their significance."

Rick Godfrey

Chapter 13. UNIONS –
"THE SECOND MANAGEMENT CHAIN"

"A vote to unionize is a vote *against* past or current management practices."

You have a union because somebody, either an individual or a group of people and management failed to treat employees as human beings with basic needs like you and me.

Having managed many unionized groups of people has taught me a ton of valuable lessons. People like fair treatment. They don't always like the outcome or the message, but if it is fair --- they can and will live with it. When things, rules, decisions, employee judgments, organizational promotions, hiring, firings, etc., don't meet the acid test of fairness --- then things in the organization come apart and don't function very well. In fact, people know when they are not being respected and treated fairly. Nobody needs to tell them or write them letters --they just know the difference between "right and wrong" when they are being managed improperly or unfairly.

One union management executive made the point to me (in fact he made great points) that company management created our operating system for managing employees, and union management modified it. He was making a very clear point which he described as: "The system ain't broke so don't fix it!" VS "The system is broke so you better fix it!" I learned a lot from this business agent. He was never afraid of working an issue with company management types like myself. All he asked was that we do it openly, and review our thinking on the solution to the problem before we took the final step and acted on the issue. Sounded good to me -- so we operated with this philosophy for a couple of years without any strikes or hard feelings. This did not mean we always agreed on the same exact solution to all problems. What it did mean was we could work on any employee problem, issue or situation without fear of reprisals from either company management or union management. These were good years for everybody.

A very significant point made to me in managing in unionized environments was that **"people are not just arms and hands" BUT, employees get treated that way by some managers. We should utilize the employee's brain as well as their hands --- because it's far more effective and you will also enjoy the working environment more.** I never met a union senior manager I didn't like and I can honestly say that I never met a concerned person I couldn't feel empathy for – whether we had a union contract or not. Someone once told me you can measure the environment of a unionized company by asking simple questions: Who's in charge of this business? Who is operating this Cafeteria? Who's in charge of the parking lot and reserved parking spaces? I say -- if you have to ask these questions your company is in trouble with its employee relations and needs immediate attention to the patient before it becomes terminal and not repairable. Said another way – examination of the answers to these questions may well give you some insight on why the union was formed and/or voted into your company in the first place. Too often management attitude towards the union is tainted and skewed by some prior managers personal view. Disregard such a bigoted opinion. Form your own experience base to operate upon. Union or non-union --- the heartbeat of the organization is still in the knowledge of the people. They know what is going on and what needs to be fixed. Park your car in the employee parking lot (not in a reserved space for managers) and talk to the employees while you walk into the office or factory. Walk the floors and listen to what people have to say about the business and their problems. Openly ask employees to make suggestions and come to you with their problems. Eat lunch in the company factory cafeteria and sit with the troops, not other managers. You will learn what needs fixing and where the issues are. Some authors have called this "Managing by walking around". This sounds good but if your eyes are closed, your ears can't hear, and your mind has already made a decision about the future course of action as a manager ----- you learn nothing. I say be open, honest, listen and look at things as others may see them and you can grow as a person and as a manager to new levels of effectiveness.

Chapter 14. CONSULTANTS
– FRIENDS OR FOE

You need to Know:

When to USE them? -- Only where they can ADD value to the business!

When NOT to use them? –- When they add NO value to the business!

The trademark of really great consultants is that they practice working their magic through others. Great managers who believe they can create positive results through others <u>also practice</u> working through others. The young manager can learn and practice the good actions by good consultants. Consultants (the good ones) know that their time of residence in any company is temporary and that things done through the current organization have a much better chance of survival than things developed by corporate "seagulls and outsiders". Europeans who are part of American corporations learned early in their organization's history that the American managers always go back to America, so they adopted a "practice" of just being patient and waited until the Americans leave and return to their homeland. The really good consultants give **ALL** the credit for successes to the permanent employees and the organizations they are interfacing with and act only as the "agent for change".

ALSO KNOW THAT:

--- Combinations of group efforts should make the individual employees' work easier. If it does not – you are probably on the wrong trail for change. Combinations of tasks should be quicker and easier not more difficult.

--- Constrictions and issues created during the use of consultants can usually be seen when the work is more difficult and expensive to accomplish. New work rules that require more signatures rather then fewer are good examples of not trusting your employees and they will resent the consultants for this new requirement. Again, you are probably on the wrong trail to any real lasting improvements.

--- Improvements gained <u>through</u> the use of regular employees will belong to the employees (and their company) – and tend to last after the consultants have departed.

--- Don't be afraid to establish <u>regularly</u> scheduled reviews with the consultants and your management team to make sure the consultants' work is being accomplished.

A unique role that consultants can play well does exist --- A great role that can be played by a truly objective consultant is one of being the person who can "tell it like it is" and they can surface issues that others in the current organization may not feel comfortable discussing openly. Usually the consultant has no political agenda, seeks no employment with the company as a permanent employee, and generally should not engage in the evaluation of permanent employees performance. Like all good rules – sometimes this rule is broken and the consultant gets into activities for which he or she is not qualified. Watch for consultants that are thinking and advising you "outside the box of their contractual specifications" that they were employed to accomplish. My one long lasting memory is of a consultant who decided (on his own) that his responsibilities included doing managerial talent reviews on behalf of his client the Division General Manager. Since the consultant was very good at doing what he was hired for (as a professional facilitator) --- his employer decided he must also be good at doing managerial performance assessments. Unfortunately he was not skilled in this field. He "cost" the General Manager and his corporation some very high talented managers (including myself) through his improper "off-hand" organizational assessments. On the other hand, since the consultant has been hired for his/her knowledge and experience - you better listen to what they have to say - even it is not in total agreement with your thinking on the subject under review. Just make sure the input is within the field of expertise of the consultant.

Caution: To Senior Managers --- or YOU, when you become a senior manager " in charge of the joint". Consultants do gravitate towards the one who hires them. Consultants think of the person signing the checks as their mentor and the person who gets all the extra silent votes on the quality of their work. Those who empower them are also those who are "first among the many" who they work for in the company or organization. I have personally seen the "demoralizing" impact of having consultants engaged by higher management making it very clear to the rest of the organization – where the direction for the consultants comes from. This can create a wall with the rest of the organization below the level of the hiring manager. To some degree this is hard to avoid but I would suggest that it's a good idea for the hiring manager to make it clear to all concerned that the consultant is NOT given a license to coerce or direct or play politics. I believe that the senior executive who is hiring the consultants owes this understanding to their permanent employees. A good short briefing to the entire management team to display the consultants authorized task in writing would be a good thing to do.

Chapter 15. CUSTOMER SERVICE

The very title of this section denotes the fact that customers do need service --- expect service --- deserve service ---and should receive service. Managers need to understand this!

If we take a customer's order on time, build and deliver their products on time and yes, even send the bill on time --- then we have successfully completed the first step in the customer service chain of life. Future relationships with this customer will play off these initial events of our first transactions with him/her. Customer memories are long --- maybe longer than that of an elephant. Negative results (and the memory of them) seem to last much longer in the archives of a disgruntled customer group. Some never forgive and forget!

Customers always talk with other potential customers. They provide the legacy you live with in your marketplaces. Customers and even competitors all talk to each other. In short, they decide your reputation and how the market you are serving will view you as a supplier. In order to properly serve your customers you need to know them extremely well. **You need feedback indicators and performance measurements to assure yourself that you are doing the job for them.** You need a customer contact plan that keeps you in touch with them even when they do not have a current order in your backlog. In short, you need to stay connected to retain the "latest views" from your markets as seen through your customer's eyes.

You also need to learn how to work **WITH** your customers as well as FOR them. Some very dynamic and productive methods include such things as "user groups", made up of a good cross-section of your active customers. We used to set-up casual sessions once or twice per year to hear directly from the customers' about their ideas on how we could improve our service. We also did this with suppliers so we could have cross-dialog on problems or issues requiring discussion on how we could work together for better results. Here suppliers and customers can give you feedback about things to do to improve your performance as a company (delivery, price, quality, product features, etc., etc.). In these sessions you can hear how you stack up against the competition, Here you can also see yourself directly through the eyes of the customer.

The customer view of "best in class" for your business segments is critical for you to understand and you should work these criteria into your formal business plans and strategies. Hearing the truth about yourself from the eyes and ears of the people who will ultimately determine if you are to become a successful company is critical for leading edge suppliers. **Now --- what is it worth to have in-site into the customers thinking about you as a supplier?**

Know these simple truths:

"Fixing customer complaints is just plain Hard Work."

"Customer perceptions are REAL ---
Especially in the customer's mind."

"It's much easier to do a great job for your customer on the first engagement ---
THAN it is to repair damage of having done a bad job on the first encounter!"

"Customers always remember how they are treated!"

Chapter 16.   MERGERS & ACQUISITIONS – MYTHS & REALITY

I remember a senior manager telling me that if a "rumored merger" took place, all our problems in the company would be solved. He was espousing the myth that the "other management team was better equipped" to manage the current business than our current senior management team who had grown up with the business. People seem to have the perpetual capacity to believe that the grass is always greener on the other side of the street and that other managers have the better ideas and approach to problem solving. Usually this turns out to be wishful thinking and dreaming of "the good times." Some people may think that the subject of mergers and acquisitions should be reserved for the senior management team. While it is true the leadership roles for these activities IS usually assigned to the senior persons--- this does not preclude younger managers from learning the valuable lessons of prompt and active action taking during the merger and acquisition process.

The real facts are that **a good merger or acquisition is like a good marriage. It has to be good for both parties.** Usually the most successful mergers occur when the deal is good for both parties. The real great marriages and mergers occur and achieve fruition when the sum of 1+1=3. In other words , putting the two entities together creates strengths born from the merger. A good merger takes the great stuff from each company and makes a new environment that is better than BOTH of the previous company processes or environments. Of course, this takes managers who are open to change and improvements – even when they did not think of the improvements themselves. Many times the culture and actions of the following activities falls to more senior managers but young managers can learn significantly from these events. Good mergers have very little room for the NIH (not invented here) factor.. ...

Managers need to carefully consider the following:

#1 --- Take actions to implement the cost savings of combining two organizations or groups as quickly as you can. Don't ignore the duplication in management, which is natural when you combine two companies or departments. Common sense says you don't need two managers to lead one combined department. Sometimes a dual departmental structure grew out of prior bad management who tried to appease everybody. Re-employ duplicate people or eliminate them. This needs to be dealt with as soon as possible and not be left to waste valuable capital and expense wages.

#2 --- A merger or acquisition is an alternative to organic growth. There are several ways to develop technologies or products to create revenue. One of the true shortcuts to a product line enhancement and market share improvement is to acquire another company that has this capability already in their product line. This can really shorten the time-to-market and develop market share leverage for your other products. Don't forget to re-set the sales targets upon completion of the merger to take advantage of the additional products and customers.

#3 --- Adopt the best practices of both organizations – don't be afraid of change or new processes and technology. Dive in fast and take advantage of this 1+1=3 opportunity.

#4 --- Cultural differences between the two organizations can be one of the biggest problems you face when putting two companies together. Remember that each company and its employees have a legacy of lessons learned on the way up the management chain or in corporate growth. Sometimes our past learning and previous environment can limit our "willingness to change". The two cultural histories may require that you hire some professional help with objectivity to solve this or formulate teams within the new company to devise solid solutions.

#5 --- Top management must first set the strategy and then align the organization behind it. Don't be bashful about personally leading these efforts or developing teams to help.

#6 --- The merger will not be completely transparent to your customers (internal and external). You will be in the spotlight through the entire process of restructuring. Develop a customer communication plan to keep them informed on your progress in merging.

#7 --- If it ain't broke ---- don't fix it!

#8 --- If <u>it</u> is broke --- turn over heaven and earth to fix it --- NOW!

#9 --- Rank all your old and new employees based on written job descriptions as soon as possible --- before you make major work assignment changes. Remember that this is NOT a personality contest to be done on hairstyle, personality, size, sex, weight and color. Real people deserve to be treated with respect and as such should be rated against real valid job criteria.

#10 --- Layoffs – These are never fun but they offer the opportunity to re-think your organization. Don't be afraid to ask for volunteers – you may be surprised to find someone who wants to be laid-off. In one of my early lay-off situations I happened to ask if anyone in my group had ideas on how we should look at the workforce reduction. To my surprise, three individuals came to me privately and volunteered for layoff.

#11 --- Many acquisitions fail because the cost savings that were identified during the euphoria of the pre-acquisition analysis slip away once the reality of post-acquisition implementation sets in. On average many acquisitions would be scored as failures when measured against their original objectives because managers rationalize themselves out of taking the tough decisions on cost reductions that are concerned with people.

Chapter 17.   STAFF WORK –

IT'S NOT FOR EVERYBODY!

Some people like staff work. For some it is an escape from decision-making. You get assignments, you dig up the facts, you develop proposals and alternatives, you present the data ---- and then someone else makes the decision on what to do and which way to go. A good example would be the decision to develop new products to fill voids in the company's product offering. You can do this through internal product development programs, you can commission another outside source to do the development, or you can buy another company who has the capability to fill your product line voids. Sometimes your materials supporting these decisions take years to come to fruition or failure. This may be the safe way to survive for some people – but not for me. **In staff work it is more important to be correct than it is to be quick** with decisions and data to support them. Others like the atmosphere of thinking out loud without risking negative feedback from results or the people affected by the decisions taken as a result of the data you present.

A real issue with staff work is to listen instead of only being constantly on "transmit". I once heard someone say:

" I can't hear you because you're talking so loud"!

Many staff people begin to think they are immortal and that they should make all major decisions on business elements even though they are not responsible for operating the business units. This is especially true in large corporations where the corporate staffers tend to reside close to the top of the company. In these situations staffers tend to think of themselves as the guardians of the corporate treasury and chief advisors to the CEO. The larger the company, the larger the staff functions and numbers of people in them. BUT – I cannot think of a single situation where the staff person was held personally accountable for the results associated with the decisions of the "line managers" – especially during the days, weeks and months **AFTER** the decision is made and implemented by line management. As line managers we live and die by the decisions we personally make and implement. Hopefully we get credit for the successful ones and some forgiveness for the minor mistakes we make as we grow.

Good staff people and good staff managers think both about the long-term potential results and impacts on the business and its people as well as the short-term affects. Another great fact is that good staff management produces helpful answers to tactical and strategic issues and not just convenient ones. Bad staff management produces more work for the organization and usually does not produce positive effects on the gross margins of the company. In short, bad staff work produces "non-value added" stuff" for others to tend to. Good staff management can be instrumental in making others successful and earns the respect of the entire organization. I love a staff manager (or staff person) who helps a line manager become successful! I had the rare experience of another peer manager giving up one of his personal objectives to help me achieve one of my departmental objectives. This was an example of putting the company's needs first and his personal objectives second. Good job Mr. Manager!

Taking a short-term manager's staff job (from your line manager's position) can be a very positive event. When you return to a line management job --- you will better appreciate the staff role and the view of the company from these jobs. Because staff jobs require extensive presentations, his assignment can also help your presentation skills as a line manager when you face staffers and executives in the future.

Personal note: **I believe staff people and their managers should be held accountable for the decisions made from their research and recommendations**. Too often the material sent to managers from staff groups is never placed in any staff employees' performance review portfolio. Too bad – maybe the quality of staff work would improve if people thought it affected their personal performance reviews and their subsequent salary treatments.

Chapter 18. FINANCIAL/OPERATIONAL PLANS VS. STRATEGIC PLANS

Everyone in the organization needs to know where he or she is going and how you plan to get there!

There are lots and lots of opinions on the value and detail levels required to have good financial and operational plans for the business. All to often, the larger the business the more formal the business plans. Some people say the larger the business the less people pay attention to the formal business planning process, except once a year when it is created for the senior management of the firm and the board of directors. Regardless of all this talk **---- I believe it is a good idea to have these annual and multi-year plans.** First, it forces you to look at yourselves as a company and focus you on your strengths or weaknesses. **Second,** it should bring to the surface the core business elements that need to be served by the organization and you as managers. **Third,** if done properly it points your focus toward the future and the needs of the company for capital, people, and technologies to support your product lines. **Fourth,** it should cause you to take stock of your competitive position in the marketplace you serve. The process is simple: set objectives; identify key and critical items required to accomplish the objectives; and finally, work out some plans and assignments of the key tasks to individuals who can lead the teams to implement these plans. Schedule periodic reviews to measure progress as required and appropriate.

For Your Information:
  Strategic plans say WHERE you are going!

  **Operational plans say HOW you plan to
  get there!**

Good planning produces good results. Solid goals
and objectives in a set of monthly plans should
produce a full year of good annual results. Sub-goals
and objectives (developed by and with your managers
and employees) usually produce even better results.
Good goals should be objectively measurable versus
subjective in nature --- do not leave measurement to
"feelings and/or perceptions". Having "no plans" can
often produce negative results. It is not unusual that
the lack of a good annual planning process allows
inventories to grow, manpower to be in a surplus
condition, receivables to increase without the
associated increases in sales and revenue, capital to be
acquired when outsourcing would have done the job -
-- without the need for more capital funds, etc, etc.
Having no business plans in medium to large size
companies almost guarantees that different
organizations in the same company will be mis-
aligned and not in-tune with the overall strategic plan.
Duplication then becomes a lodestone and corrective
actions by managers becomes more difficult. Under
these conditions, if you are not having fun then you
better find out why and correct these out-of-control
processes. The lack of good plans usually provides a
lack of focus for employees and the company in
general.

Unfocused companies can end up being "Out of business companies"!

Strategic Planning – is both a process and a product designed to promote communication and understanding of where the ship is going. Done properly it creates a stronger institution capable of moving more rapidly forward toward the company's mission to reach its desired levels of service and performance. This planning process is known as "Disciplined Creativity" according to Rick Daley of the EMD Consulting Group in Sedona, AZ. He says, "a great mission statement does not replace a good strategic plan"!

Good strategic planning also makes you get a picture of your environment -- thereby forcing you to focus on real issues and real competition.

Chapter 19.   MANAGEMENT BEHAVIOR

"RICK-ISMS" FOR YOUR USE

There are many ways to characterize managers and their management styles. It is extremely important that each of us realize how we are perceived by other people, other managers, customers and all their organizations. The following views (Rick-isms) also tend to place each manager into a profile that affects how he or she will be given future assignments by bosses in charge of their career placements. In short, some of our many career opportunities are affected by how we act and are perceived to act as a manager today. Some of the following categories may fit each of us but all of them have some importance and affect our successes or failures as a manager.

YOU CHOOSE THE ITEMS THAT FIT YOUR PERSONAL SITUATION:

Ego Related
Quit trying to convince people that you are a bigger shot than you are!

Quit hogging all the credit for success. Give it to your organization and associates --- where you know it belongs.

Quit trying to impress the world with an office, rugs, paintings & furniture.

Remember a bit of humility in a big shot is very attractive and impressive.

Quit thinking that a bit of success in one industry qualifies you to be an expert in all fields of endeavor.

Quit dreaming of being a fast-expanding genius whiz kid and go to work. Dreams do blow-up from time to time.

Get the chip off your shoulder------it will be easier to carry the rest of the load.

Laugh every day. If you have nothing to laugh about then go look in the mirror. It is a sure laugh.

Hiring Related

Avoid the pressure to hire less competent relatives or personal friends. They do not always make the most objective employees.

Remember your payroll is your biggest expense - You pay people for their participation - don't waste any of it.

There are "book smarts" and then there are "street smarts". Don't discount people who make the right decisions without any fancy formal education credentials or certificates.

People Related

Remember that people are human beings with pride, hope, fears, and ambitions, --- & their individual packages come with good traits and bad traits.

Average Americans exert only 75% of their potential. With inspirational leadership, they can rise above the average.

You pay people for their participation --- Don't waste it.

Negative energy created at the water cooler or coffee machine takes 6 months to repair.

Profits are in the hands of the employees ---- If they trust the management and feel the company is fair, production will increase. If they feel neglected and suspicious, production will fall over time.

A contented and competent workforce with confidence in management's integrity and fairness is a great sales force.

High IQ and good judgment are two different things. Judgment comes from trying – failing – and then trying again with persistence. Remember your creative people are the most sensitive -- don't crush ideas, crazy or sensible.

Focus Related
Take care of your current job and the next one will take care of itself.

Applaud managers who give their employees credit for legitimate successes and accept responsibility/accountability for all the failures as their own.

Quit being a detail bug --- you don't have the time --- and nobody likes it anyway.

Delegate all of your responsibilities except for inspiration, accountability, and the final decisions.

Role Related
Don't forget that your job is to draw out the good traits and overcome the bad traits by the Golden Rule, inspirational leadership, and constant communication.

Practice complete personal integrity. --- Even if you lose the business.

Don't mix business and pleasure.

Remember you don't pay the payroll --- Your customers do.

Balance Related
Serve your job, community, and country – but – never to the extent of neglecting your family

In small disputes – err on the generous side for the other position. Don't plan to fight to the death over trivial matters.

Planning Related
Learn that good labor relations are a matter of head and heart, not legal rights. Fire your labor lawyer – if he/she carries a rules book around with all the answers.

Embrace an employee relations department that helps managers solve problems instead of quoting the personnel policy book.

Take time to step back and look at the big picture and not just your department.

Get out of the weeds ---- think outside of the traditional box for your job.

Plan your organization to use eight hours of your workers "head power and thinking" as well as the eight hours of their hands.

Often good luck is due to preparation. Make plans to win when the breaks go for you AND against you. Most good business decisions result not from luck, but from getting the facts and having the foresight to plan well.

Constantly and honestly review your progress. If you need to make tough changes --- make them yourself or your successor will do it for you.

Always suspect that a period of trouble may be ahead --- so maintain a reserve to cover it.

Run your organization or company lean and hungry -- even in boom times.

Learning Related
Don't reorganize your newly assigned management group before you know what's going on.

Don't assume your new organization has the same culture as your old one.

Communications Related

Keep your office door open to all employees. When they have the "open door" privilege they seldom can find things to complain about.

Just because your office door is open does not mean you have earned the managerial element called "trust" with all your employees. Some people will never walk through the door!

Mix and listen. -- Then you will know what your staff and employees are thinking.

Eat regularly in the company café WITH the troops – they can teach you a lot about your business and its needs.

Remember everybody's name.

Chapter 20. JOBS I HAVE LOVED ---
NAME THEM AND REMEMBER WHY!

It is my hope that these small **vignettes** can provide something in a positive manner to **show that new managers can survive in tough places.** Many of our growth experiences are not the easy type of "no hassle environments" we dream about for our first management job:

Supervision 101

My very first "first line supervisors job" was in a union environment and a strange product group. Boy, was I ever lucky to land this job and be exposed to the learning and teaching from it. Philadelphia was the town. A large well-respected electronics company was the place. The IBEW was the union. "Bernie" was my mentor. The order file was full of good customers. The job was production control supervision. The job situation called for improving results in "on-time product delivery." How could I pass up this job with all that it could teach me!

Three years -- three months and three days after arriving on the scene in the factory I had risen a couple of levels, moved into a much larger part of the company and was engaged in the international operations of this company. My employees showed me where to look in solving the major problems. They also contributed heavily to this success and the creation of the new opportunities. All this and they paid me too! My managerial growth and learning curves were ascending "straight up" -- exponentially.

No place in the world could have provided a better learning experience for me as a young manager. In the beginning the customers screamed over the phones, the directors were unhappy with the delivery performances from all our factories, employees were being treated unfairly, management had ducked the issues of proper tooling and equipment, suppliers delivered what they wanted - when they wanted to deliver it, and among all this was the field of opportunity to learn --- and by the way, the union was trying to run the company. **WOW** – what a great place to learn!!!!

I was fortunate enough to have a solid, never tiring, always listening and supportive boss called "Bernie" who grew up in the East coast company cultures. He had a feeling for the people in the organization, the union environment that we lived in and never seemed to go home at night. I was also lucky to have employees that were hungry for change and willing to put themselves "out on a limb" to make improvements in our processes. We managed delivery schedules, kept senior managers from re-arranging schedules and priorities in the factory daily, included the union management in decisions affecting ALL the factory employees, and dozens of other things were overhauled and improved. We also restarted proper employee relation activities in the critical area of communications. Employees also improved the planning and provisioning systems that all employees used to operate the factory. As managers all we asked in return for these investments was a "fair days work for a fair days pay from each and every employee".

This job was the greatest learning process that I can ever remember in my young management years. Sometimes the worst environments are the best teachers for new managers. Sometimes the most difficult working situations provide the greatest opportunity to learn and excel as a manager. These tough jobs teach you the most important lessons on how to manage people the fastest. Boy, these lessons learned stay with you forever in your working career!

Schiphol -- Amsterdam, Holland
Industrial Spare Parts

Early in my management career the opportunity to manage a special project came to me as an international assignment. The Industrial Products Division in this major American corporation had a real problem providing customers with on-time spare parts deliveries. Since we provided industrial marketplace with continuous process flow instrumentation our products could not be out of service very long before the customers revenues were substantially affected.

For years the European subsidiaries had horded their worldly share of spare parts and refused to share their inventories with the other European subsidiaries of the same company. The English would never send spare parts to France, etc., etc. At the same time the supplying factories would rather build and ship complete new products than provide spare parts of lesser value for the old ones. Finally, the corporate executives became embroiled enough with disgruntled customers that they decided to fix this problem. They assembled and chartered a team of American and European mid-level managers and requested a solution be proposed to fix this problem. I was fortunate enough to be invited to participate.

This chartered five-person team met for long hours and after several days concluded that the "right approach to fix this problem" was clear but would be almost impossible to implement because of nationalistic cultural and corporate score-keeping reasons. The bottom line was that we felt no European General Manager would participate willingly in our recommended solution for four major reasons: 1- His personal performance would be degraded and therefore his compensation would be affected; 2- He would not want his customers to receive parts from another European subsidiary where he had no personal control of the product deliveries; 3- He did not trust the other General Managers to perform effectively on his behalf; 4- the original idea was not his.

The "right approach" recommended solution was simple and clear. We needed to consolidate all the spare parts that sat in 16 subsidiaries through out Europe into one quick turn-around logistics operation. These parts could be shipped directly from the factories in bulk, held in bond in the logistics center, and then shipped in small quantities on demand to the customers' over-night (mostly by air since spare parts on industrial instrumentation tends to be very small and light). This new center could provide guaranteed service in 3-5 days instead of the historical 1-3 months (which was always depending on factory availability). The cost and performance of the unit would be reviewed monthly just like the other subsidiaries and be done with the European General Managers on a monthly basis. The General Managers' court of appeal, if they were not happy with the service or performance records, was at the corporate level. The financial favorable impact to the corporation and its associated savings were estimated and drawn up as requirements for implementation. We estimated reductions in inventory targets, increase in service performance to customers goals, and "not to exceed costs" to operate the facility. We also recommended it be put in a free-trade zone, under bond, on Amsterdam's Schiphol Airport Facilities in Holland (neutral territory where you paid no duties until you withdrew the goods and shipped to a specific customer). We suggested it be run by the Dutch and staffed with technical personnel so goods could be shipped to customers directly and then billed on invoices which bore the subsidiary companies sales credit name. The only "kicker" in the solution was that the corporation needed to authorize a one-time write-off of the obsolete inventories that had built up in each of the subsidiaries over the years of hording spare parts – and -- not charge the General Managers personal performance review with this multi- million dollar loss.

We proposed this recommended solution to the then CEO (who had issued our charter to recommend a solution) of the corporation and his staff (including the group vice-president for international operations). The CEO agreed to the entire recommendation and personally volunteered to participate in the announcement of the program in the General Management Annual Meeting. His participation was critical to dispel any feelings and thoughts that this project was "up for a vote by the European managers". Since I was making the presentation to him (by choice of our team), I was delighted when he gave his approval for the entire project (as recommended) and then was shocked to be asked by him if I could/would run this project. Of course I said YES and was moved to the corporate offices as the new project manager. Wow, another continuation in my learning process and growth experiences!

Colorado -- a "High Country Fix-it"

This was a turn-around that saved major customers and corrected the financial performance of a division within a corporation. Marketers had sold the customers on these wonderful new products – that were "not quite through their development process yet". Hundreds of sales were made with no completely designed product to produce and deliver. **WOW**, what an opportunity to learn!

The general manager and several directors were replaced and some of us chosen as the new managers were given the opportunity to try and fix-it. Four years later – all was well, and several of us had learned new and valuable lessons on selling products before the engineers were through with their work. Several of us also learned (the hard way) about not releasing product to the factories (and customers) before the final testing and evaluations are complete in engineering. And, finally, most of us learned about union organization campaigns when the employees are feeling management pressure to do something that is not quite physically possible (like when the factory is asked to build hardware that is still in the design stages of development).

> *"The acquisition of your dreams!*
> *- Or –*
> *A New England company invaded by a*
> *Midwest corporation manager"*

My first President's job and joy occurred in this assignment. This major division of a Midwest electronics firm acquired a small family-owned company to enhance the division's current product line. Acquisition was done instead of using internal product development teams to design products to fill the product line gaps.

I arrived on the job of the acquired company to be CEO just as an economic recession began in the industrial market places of the United States. This marketplace held the customer base that we served as our primary product users. Our backlogs went from being flush with customer orders, and building a new plant to a situation where my secretary and I opened the mail each morning to review the new customer orders for the week. Too many people, too much inventory, no new products, and an old business environment purchased from the previous family owners who had sold it to a corporation before their children ran it into the ground. OUCH – another great opportunity to learn!

We wrote a new business plan after several months of examining the competition, the market place, our capabilities and a deep look at all the technologies available to us as a small company within the parent corporation. We were lucky -- we restructured and re-engineered the product lines with modern technologies and manufacturing processes, we offered the customers never before seen product capabilities and we built them at reasonable costs through streamlined manufacturing processes. It all turned out to be very successful, and growth and profits followed for the employees and our corporation. The only people not happy with our performance were the competitors. We took over the majority market share and beat the competition to the European market too. Oh well, you can please some of the people some of the time but you can't please all the competition all the time.

German Turn-around
An opportunity to manage in another culture – Theirs!

If you have ever worked in Europe you know how close all the borders and cultures are to each other. You also know that some cultures are more structured than others. This environment was one where the company had always been successful and never had to face a major product failure or market place rejection of their technology. In short -- the management team had always had it pretty easy when it came to the operation of the business.

Suddenly a significant new product line failed after market introduction and installation into the customer's product. OUCH – another opportunity to learn how to keep the customer, fix the installed base of our product and re-train your organization on proper product development, test, and evaluation. On top of all this the European company culture had a terrible time admitting it had made some mistakes in its management of its people. Additionally, the internal human resources organization did not want to accept help from outside the business unit --- even though they were part of a much larger corporation with many resources. We withdrew the product, went back through major product testing, and re-engineered the manufacturing processes to build and deliver the newly tested hardware to the customer.

Two years later we again had a happy (but more cautious) customer and in addition we had a newly trained managerial group that proudly exhibited their new managerial skills. We also had a new Human Relations Director. The old director never could adjust to change and having employee involvement in managing their own processes in engineering and manufacturing.

Italian Turn-around – A lesson in a European family-owned company acquired by an American corporation.

Interesting situations are developed by American companies who purchase European companies – they leave them completely alone to operate their businesses -- and then are surprised when they get into trouble through over-expansion or entering into a business that they know nothing about managing. Product lines were old (some designed by the father of the then current general manager), the products had old technologies and the customers were heavily bound by tradition on product selection and application. When the customer decided to modernize their products they produced specifications that required suppliers to use unproven and/or unfamiliar technologies. These new technology infusions introduced major risk in the product lines in both application and the life of the products. On top of this, the internal research and development budgets were not adequate for such an ambitious new technology product line push. And -- the revenue enjoyed by this company was not sufficient to digest a 3-5% financial impact hit of total revenue in the current operating 2-3 year product development cycles. So where did we go to solve this equation?

We went through a total product line "value analysis" of the entire business. We screened all existing products for gross and net margin contribution and re-priced the low contributors. We eliminated some product lines that had no future, re-engineered the factory processes for lean manufacturing opportunities, and developed a strategic supplier set of relationships for the future. It worked -- but it took two years to get it all done. Today the father of the General Manager is happily retired, the son is happy not having the father looking over his shoulder every day, the customers think well of the company, and the employees and managers have a great continuing education process to keep themselves sharp and alert for future product opportunities. Oh yes, they have significantly increased the product output of the organization without significant increases in added employees to accomplish this through a better business structure.

France --a two-company combination – And a profitable turn-around!!

Completion of the overall operational plan took less than one year! Completion of the combination of the two operating companies took another year. This is one of my favorites – the favorite of learning lessons and jobs. Putting two companies together successfully is no small task. Doing it in France as an American under French labor laws makes it even more exciting and challenging. You can imagine the duplication of organizational elements that existed in the two companies. Many times you have really good employees doing the same functions in both companies. What do you do with two really good employees when you only need one to manage the new business? This is the type of question faced in these combinations. We promoted one and retrained the other in an equally important job in another part of the organization.

The business planning for the future becomes one huge task, especially when it is coupled with keeping the business running correctly under these very unusual and difficult circumstances of combining the companies. New organizational structures, selection of managers to run the new functions, assessment of the financial assets and resources to run the "new company", developing a customer notifications plan, creating the physical floor plans for the company, developing a roadmap for the sequencing of the relocations and combinations all take considerable effort.

To accomplish this we deeply involved the "new managers" who would be running the future company in the design and development of the new organization configuration and its structures. They were given guidelines on affordable cost levels and expectations of the performance levels required for the "new company". With these "guidelines" in-hand they developed a new strategic plan and built an operations set of objectives for themselves. This pre-planning took considerable effort but allowed each manager to exercise his/her personal preferences and opinions on how to operate their portion of the company.

This freedom of choice and expression of personal management philosophy turned out to be one of the most critical steps in establishing a new culture within the new company. From this point forward every new manager was learning, teaching and sharing their lifetime business knowledge with the other new managers. What we developed through this process was the strongest teamwork that either previous company had ever experienced. Managers began to give up personal turf and old standards while they developed the new processes by which they chose to do their work. Since some employees were moved across functions to do the best job possible, old barriers came down and new strengths rose to the surface of the new organization.

This entire planning process took twelve months to complete. The new company took another year to become a reality. "Networking" became an every day occurrence between the managers. Up, down, sideways, and even some people sought outside advice in how they could most effectively manage this new company. Surplus employees were dealt with openly and fairly – some scheduled for departure even volunteered to assist the employees that would remain with the company for short-term employment. Others were quickly given new assignments.

The mother corporation was the most impetuous and anxious player in the development process. They (the corporate management folks) needed to be "managed" so they did not interfere with our normal local management team. We did not need any corporate "seagulls" flying around and dropping needless tasks on the individuals trying to do their new jobs. Since the guy in charge of this project was an outspoken American (me) --- the process proceeded without too much interruption and intervention by all the "interested parties" from the United States. Later, one of the most senior human resource corporate executives told me he was glad we kept them at bay. He felt this was a key in allowing the new management team to "own" their chosen organizations' structures and the processes by which they successfully ran the businesses. Thank goodness for small favors!

Chapter 21.   SURVIVAL TIPS
FOR THE NEW MANAGERS

Somebody once said --- survival is an art. I say
**"performance is the art of doing things like you
said you would do them".** If you perform --
wonderful stuff happens to you—you survive! You
get promoted, you get to continue to receive your
paycheck, you can come back tomorrow and work
another day, you can keep your medical insurance,
you can eat, ------ you get the picture! We all know
there is no such thing as a "free lunch". You earn
whatever you get in this world. Only a limited few
have someone who hands them a free lunch in their
lifetime.   Sooooo --- now that we have the rules
straight, what can we do to survive in this competitive
job market? I say "cover yourself in the art of doing
things as you promised to do them". Keep your
commitments, keep your word, and help another
manager achieve his/her objectives. Keep your hands
out of other peoples' pockets, and spend time
improving your own individual performance – not
worrying about another person's situation. Carry
your share of the load --- and maybe a little of the
next person's, too. Do all these things well and your
next career job will appear by itself.

Some managers who fail to survive -- do so because
they never trusted anyone. They tried to always be the
one with the correct answers. They never shared an
idea with an employee or their peers, or even their
boss. They just implemented their ideas without
testing them with anybody. No wonder their boss
was shocked when they put him/her crossways with

their peers. **You can't have ALL the right answers ALL the time**. When we were new young managers we were happy batting 60-70% --- right? Later we learned that most major league hitters never ever achieve this level of performance. This would be the equivalent of getting 6 or 7 base hits out of every 10 trips to the plate for the entire season. That's one of the reasons why being a manager is such a tough job. Never the less, if you treat yourself like an all-star and play like an all-star, you will probably exceed your own personal expectations.

Finding mentors helps you as a manager, but that means you need to communicate with someone whose opinion or experience you value and trust. There is that word trust again. You earn that by the way you treat people. Remember managers are people too, so trust them when they earn the right to be trusted. It will be a less lonely managerial life for you.

Tip: Mentors can be peers too!

Changing positions or operations, versus changing companies is a tool that managers and employees sometimes overlook. Some people jump from company to company looking for whatever they dream about or can think about as paradise. It rarely occurs to these people that you have companies within your current company. Sometimes just changing department's scratch's an itch you may have for change. If your company is a good one, and many of them really are good companies – then they deserve a chance to address a good employees' issue or problem and/or desires for change before you lose them. Of course, this action of communicating requires you to talk with your boss about your particular situation or the employee needs to talk with you to make this a positive change. Once again you or your employee are required to trust someone.

Remember, during periods of change:

> **"Until peoples' personal needs are satisfied -- people don't always pay attention to all the important stuff in a business."**

> **"Treat individual people the same way you wish to be treated and they will respond to you as their manager."**

> **"Your company's reputation reflects your personal business practices – as does yours, too."**

> **"Shareholder companies are all in business to make a profit" – Remember-- this is your responsibility as a manager to oversee this focus! Don't lose it!**

> **"Working 16-18 hours a day keeps managers away from their families. Remember – there is a need for balance between personal life and business life. If either gets too far out of balance then both lose their perspective!"**

Chapter 22. SELF-APPRAISAL PROCESS

Maybe the parting shot in this text is **"helpful hints to and for hopeful managers"** and should be on the subject of self-appraisal. It is sometimes easier to talk about the other person rather than looking in the mirror and taking stock of one's own self. Many of us are good (or think we are) at giving advice but few of us can stop and be very objective about ourselves. Our own behavior, including the supervision of others, needs review on a regular basis. **Things change --- do we change with them? Some of us keep on working with the same old tools and principles. Tools that lose their edge and principles that were written in some other time period --- not today – may not be very effective in the current environment.**

Sources of useful information for self-appraisal are:
Spouse or other family members (especially children)
Your professional association fellow-managers
Internal company customers
Your employees
Your boss

We all have goals, expectations and plans for the future. If they come true – OK. But, what if they do not meet our expectations? How does not achieving your goals affect your employees? How does this affect other departments, managers or organizations? Sometimes our inability to achieve our personal expectations as a manager has long reaching impacts. Distrust of others, distrust of our employees, and distrust of our own capabilities can (if not managed) lead to degradation of the environment in your own organization.

Sooooo – get hold of your emotions and move out to correct any deficiencies in the culture. Don't let personal disappointments infect and erode your department's performance. The same goes for your employees. When you see people getting "down" on themselves your job is to get into the core of the problem with the employee and solve the issue if it is work related. Employees failing to meet their own personal expectations can quickly lead to other employees also fearing some personal loss.

Surveys -- *r*emember this about a public reviewing of your management style (I say public because anything done in a survey on this subject matter never stays private) ---**people expect change and results from <u>any</u> type of survey.** Expectations in the workforce that something will change as a result of the survey is "a given with most people". Some folks (me among them) say -- don't start an employee opinion survey that you are not prepared to answer with all the employees. You may not expect to take action to cure their ills – but – your employees expect it!

> *Oh, by the way* – you do know that departed employees stay in-touch with the current folks on the payroll. Your audience is larger than you think it is!

> *Helpful hints* for new supervisors: Short-term (< 1 year) employees give information more freely than longer-term folks.

Protect the messengers --Remember your management team perceives that some interviews are threatening.

Ask yourself what could (not should) be done to correct your imperfections as a manager without a survey!

Take stock of yourself regularly. ---- Do it yourself!

HOW TO CLOSE THIS DISCUSSION?

With this Postscript!

Maybe some of my personal thoughts about being a manager for years and years would be of value!

I have never regretted getting into the role and the responsibilities of being a manager.

I always felt I could be a better manager --- but not by myself. I needed every one of my employees helping to make things successful and productive.

I regularly found that employees know what needs to be done to improve the processes, the organization, the company and the total business. You only need to gain their trust in order for them to share it with you as a manager.

I have always known that my employees were the ones who made me successful. They were the critical assets that pushed me into larger and larger responsibilities. They were the key to exceeding even my own expectations as a manager! They were always my most important assets in any job I held as a manager --- at any level in the companies for which I worked.

Gauge your personal accomplishment "report card" with a small, simple and clear measurement --- A *Performance Yardstick*

++++++++++++++++++++

PERFORMANCE: is the "art" of doing things like you said you would do them! - Rick

++++++++++++++++++++

How is your managerial performance???

Still want to be a manager???

Step into the spotlight!!!

Take Charge!!!

+++++++

Good Luck! ------- Rick

ACKNOWLEDGMENTS:

"The Kids" – Pamela Godfrey Scalia, Eric Godfrey, Greg Godfrey -- For prodding and encouragement to produce this book.

"My Best Friend" -- Nan Godfrey for the hours of proofing and encouragement to write this document. Also, for the patience while I was doing the writing.

To other friends who were "The First-time Readers" for their willingness to be candid on the books content and sharing their perspective about the needs of future readers as managers.

Kjell Andersson	David Brader
Jeff Calkins	Sam Carlson
Gene Collet	Jim Coulter
Aaron Elkins	Charlotte Elkins
Ed Elko	Jim/Judy Flanders
Mildred Fox	Ken Fujino
Andre Gold	Eric Godfrey
Greg Godfrey	James Godfrey
Roy Herman	Lloyd Hightower
Leonard Hirschfeld	Bill Hubbard
Don Kovar	Jack Lord
Woody Myers	Kelly O'Mera
Pepper Putnam	Joe Sacha
Terry Samphire	Pamela Scalia
Tom Whisman	Jim Wogsland

Reader Comments

Aaron Elkins - Author - Mystery Writer--I felt like I was talking with you and listening to your messages in person.

Bill Hubbard - American President Lines - Sr. Vice President - I wish I had this book as a kid manager starting out in business.

Dave Brader - Washington State University -- "This is a Primer for managers" - This brings to mind the quotation: Eagles fly above and alone.

Don Kovar - TRW Corporate Vice President - Retired "This is not meant to be a compendium of everything a person needs to know to be a manager. Rather, it is a personal account, based on decades of experience of a set of lessons that you have learned that might be useful to someone just starting out in a management career."

Ed Elko - AEROJET-Ordnance Co. -President Retired "Excellent lessons learned and very well presented. I want copies for my kids."

Gary Michels - Best Western Motel Owner -For any prospective managerial seeking person this would be very helpful to avoid the pitfalls most usually encountered.

Gene Collet - Body Shop Business Owner - Retired - Enjoyed this book very much and would recommend it to everyone who wants to be in supervision.

Jack Lord - Advertising Executive Retired - Powerful and very knowledgeable.

Jim Godfrey - DuPont - Global Director, Operations - Really useful and interesting. I like the style and content.

Jeff Calkins - MRI Consulting Co - President -Rick Godfrey has been successful in a wide variety of interesting and challenging leadership positions during his distinguished career. As someone fortunate enough to have worked for and with Rick for 20 years, I have seen first-hand how he consistently puts into practice a positive leadership philosophy, winning outlook, and effective coaching style to achieve organizational goals while developing new leaders. This book provides the aspiring leader with the essence of what it takes to succeed in his or her chosen journey.

Jim Coulter - Chevron - Retired Finance Executive - I wish I had a copy of this when I first became a supervisor.

Jim Wogsland - Caterpillar Co-Chairman - Retired - This book is an easy read with a lot of good pointers to being a manager. "This is real MBWA (Managing by walking around)."

Joe Sacha - Vice President MRI - Consulting Co. -Ohio -I think you have a winner here! Where were you when I was 25? Now I can only reflect back.

Jim/Judy Flanders - Independent Retail Business Owner -I particularly appreciate your belief that "you should follow though and do what you say you are going to do"----this applies to management and life!

Kelly O'Mera - SunLand Golf & CC - Head Golf Professional -There is some great stuff here and I am sure it will help me do a better job as a manager.

Ken Fujino - TransAmerica Insurance-Division President Retired -You have a knack of taking things that many people consider a science and convey it in practical living terms - common sense.

Kjell A. Andersson - Chairman of the Board, Wildbats Networks, Inc (former VP & General Manager of Ericsson Radio Systems, AB - Sweden) - I find the book very useful for anyone interested in the views of an experienced executive having moved through all the ranks during his active job life. It is short and to the point and as soon as I sat down to read it -- I could not stop until I had finished it.

Leonard Hirschfeld - Financial Management -This is a solid, thought-provoking piece that delivers real value for "aspiring", "new" and "not so new" managers. I like your straight-forward writing style.

Pam Scalia - Senior Buyer - National Instruments - I have used the draft of this book over and over in everyday applications and I love the success I get from using it. I keep it easily accessible on the corner of my desk! It is wonderful to see all your wisdom and experience in print.

Roy Herman - Faculty Member - Graduate School of Business - University of Wisconsin. "If I was still teaching this book would be mandatory reading for all my graduate business school classes".

Sam Carlson - Kaiser Aerospace - President Electronic Processor Group Retired - I certainly agree with the "lessons learned that you are passing on. Chapter 19 could become Poor Richard's Almanac for Managers".

Terry Samphire - Boeing - Senior Manager - Retired - Rick's book is an excellent "toolbox" for the aspiring manager. It also provides a superb reference for the established manager.

Tom Whisman - Consultant - My compliments on a very well written, compact book of excellent advice and action items – for those who are managers, want to be managers or even those who chose to be "individual contributors" in organizations today.

Woody Myers - Sears Retired - I have been a manager and I wish I had your book available at that time. WOW, what a time saver your book would have been. I think of it as the business bible and like the holy bible should be used daily.

www.ingramcontent.com/pod-product-compliance
Lightning Source LLC
Chambersburg PA
CBHW022022170526
45157CB00003B/1319